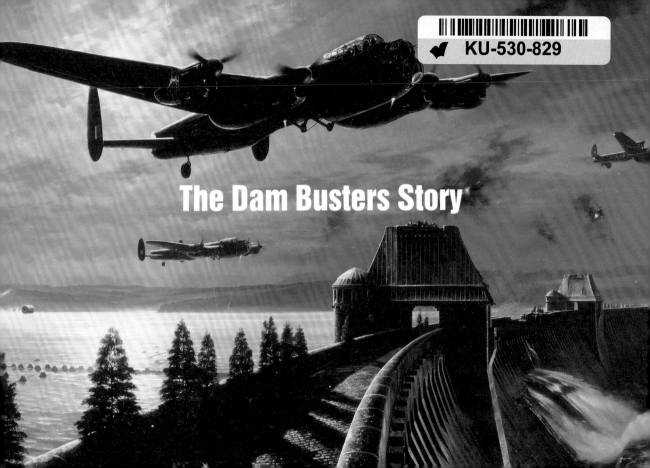

The Dam Busters Story

*Wg Cdr Guy Gibson's
Lancaster at low level
during Upkeep weapon
trials at Reculver in May
1943.* (IWM FLM2348)

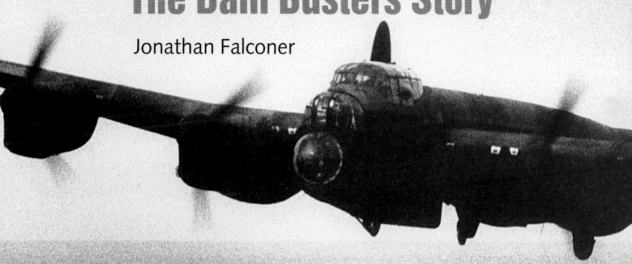

The Dam Busters Story

Jonathan Falconer

Sutton Publishing

➤
Lancaster ED817/G took part in the Upkeep dropping trials at Reculver on 20 April 1943. (Bruce Robertson collection)

Half title page:
Wg Cdr Guy Gibson and Flt Lt Mick Martin use their Lancasters to draw enemy fire away from Flt Lt 'Dinghy' Young's aircraft as he releases his Upkeep weapon over the Möhne lake.
(From an original painting by Nicolas Trudgian – www.nicolastrudgian.com)

First published in the United Kingdom in 2007 by
Sutton Publishing Limited · Phoenix Mill
Thrupp · Stroud · Gloucestershire · GL5 2BU

Copyright © Jonathan Falconer, 2007

Jonathan Falconer has asserted the moral right to be identified as the author of this work.

British Library Cataloguing in Publication Data
A catalogue for this book is available from the British Library.

ISBN 978-0-7509-4758-9

Typeset in 9.5/14.5pt Syntax.
Typesetting and origination by
Sutton Publishing Limited.
Printed and bound in England.

CONTENTS

ACKNOWLEDGEMENTS

I would like to thank the following for their kind permission to reproduce images in this book: Nicolas Trudgian (www.nicolas trudgian.com); Imperial War Museum; RAF Museum; TRL Ltd; Bundesarchiv, Germany; Canal Plus; Eder-Touristic, Germany; Mike Cawsey, Mike Garbett and Brian Goulding; Martin Latham; Peter R. March; Paul Couper; Dr Alfred Price; the late Bruce Robertson; Richard Simms; Bow Watkinson. Thanks are also due to Jane Hutchings, Anne Bennett and Glad Stockdale at Sutton Publishing for their contributions towards the editorial and design aspects of this book.

Pieces of masonry are scattered along the roadway atop the Möhne dam. In the centre can be seen the huge breach in the dam wall. (Bundesarchiv)

Ground crew at work on the port outer Rolls-Royce Merlin engine of an Avro Lancaster. (IWM TR20)

The daring attack on the Ruhr dams in May 1943 by RAF Lancasters of 617 Squadron remains one of the greatest aviation feats of the twentieth century. It has all the ingredients of a classic adventure story: the use of a miracle weapon designed to destroy an indestructible target; and the raid itself carried out by an elite bomber squadron led by a young commander at the peak of his profession.

The operation – codenamed Chastise – was only made possible by the unprecedented co-operation of a team of men and women drawn from across the political, scientific and military communities. That it happened at all was largely due to the tenacity and vision of two individuals: Dr Barnes Wallis and Air Chief Marshal Sir Charles Portal. It was Wallis who invented the revolutionary bouncing bomb, and Portal,

the Chief of the Air Staff, who saw its potential and overruled the objections of Air Chief Marshal Sir Arthur 'Bomber' Harris, giving the go-ahead for the operation.

One hundred and thirty-three RAF airmen set forth in nineteen specially modified Lancaster bombers on the evening of 16 May, their targets the great dams of western Germany. Using their bouncing bombs they succeeded in destroying two out of the three principal targets, the Möhne and the Eder dams, and badly damaging the third, the Sorpe. Floodwaters of biblical proportions were unleashed along the Ruhr valley, disrupting transport and industry and claiming the lives of more than 1,200 people.

Eight Lancasters and fifty-six airmen failed to return from Chastise, making it one of the RAF's most costly operations of the war.

In the years that have followed the raid,

◄◄
Wg Cdr Guy Gibson with four of his crew who flew on the dams raid. From left to right: Wg Cdr Guy Gibson, Plt Off Fred Spafford, Flt Lt Bob Hutchison, Plt Off George Deering and Flg Off Torger Taerum. (IWM TR1127)

opinion about its strategic value among historians and commentators on both sides has been divided. Whichever view you support, the fact remains that the bravery, skill and sacrifice of the crews of 617 Squadron is unquestionable. This is their story and the story, too, of the bouncing bomb and its inventor, Barnes Wallis.

Jonathan Falconer
Bradford-on-Avon
October 2006

'For extraordinary courage, exceptional leadership and example in the face of the enemy over three and a half years of hazardous operations culminating in the successful attacks on the Möhne and Eder dams, which he personally led and wherein he displayed, as is usual with him, the highest valour in the face of deliberately sought and tremendous additional risk, this officer is most strongly recommended for the award of the Victoria Cross.'

Extract from recommendation for immediate award of Victoria Cross to Wing
Commander Guy Gibson

➤
The Möhne dam pictured before the Second World War. (Crown Copyright)

Did You Know?
In 1939 Barnes Wallis was assistant chief designer of the Aviation Section at Vickers-Armstrong, Weybridge. He had already made a name for himself as designer of the R100 airship, and the Wellesley and Wellington bombers.

Before the Second World War, the Air Ministry had investigated the possibility of attacking with aircraft the great dams in western Germany that fed water to the factories and foundries of the Ruhr. Vast reservoirs in the upper reaches of the Rivers Ruhr and Eder stored water that was vital to heavy industry, domestic water supplies, flood protection and water management. The biggest of these dams were the Möhne and the Sorpe, which provided 75 per cent of the Ruhr's water requirements, and the Eder, which was vital to flood prevention in the Hessen region. If they could be destroyed in time of war, it would have a devastating effect on German industry as well as morale.

To be effective, any attack on the dams would need to be mounted in the spring, when the water flow was at its greatest. But experience had shown that narrow structures like dam walls were difficult targets to hit from above. They were also resistant to destruction from conventional bombing attacks.

Dams are enormous concrete or masonry structures set on broad bases with high walls, and triangular in cross-section to give them strength. They are almost invulnerable to direct hits from bombs or the effect of shock waves. Thus, the great challenge that faced Air Ministry planners was how to mount a successful attack.

For some time, a British inventor named Barnes Wallis had been working on the problem of how to breach the dams. In 1939, tests were carried out at the Road Research Laboratory in Harmondsworth into the poss-ibilities for destroying dams. Wallis discussed these tests with the director, Sir William Glanville, and his team. In October 1940 the

Did You Know?

The largest dam in western Germany was the Eder, which held back 202 million cubic metres of water. Contrary to many accounts of the dams raid, the Eder is not in the Ruhr valley. It had no link to Ruhr industry and was used for water management.

1

the Director of Scientific Research at the Ministry of Aircraft Production (MAP). He allowed Wallis to use the Road Research Laboratory to test the effects of explosive charges when placed against or near the wall of a gravity-type dam like the Möhne and Eder. Further trials involving a one-fiftieth scale model of the Möhne dam and a full-size dam in mid-Wales proved that the Möhne

first in a series of trials was carried out on a scale model of the Möhne dam to see whether a big conventional bomb could destroy it. The results were not encouraging and the Air Ministry lost interest.

But Wallis refused to give up. His latest theory found a receptive mind in Dr D.R. Pye,

'Early in 1942, I had the idea of a missile, which if dropped on the water at a considerable distance upstream of the dam would reach the dam in a series of ricochets, and after impact against the crest of the dam would sink in close contact with the upstream face of the masonry.'

Barnes Wallis

could be breached if 6,500lb of high explosive could be detonated against the inner wall of the dam. A key factor in the success of these tests was to ensure that the explosive charge was placed up against the dam wall.

So Wallis set his mind to the problem. He concluded that when the charge was detonated, the resulting shock waves would crack open the structure and allow the massive back-pressure of millions of gallons of water to finish the job.

A one-fiftieth scale model of the Möhne dam, painstakingly constructed at the Building Research Station at Garston, near Watford. (TRL Ltd)

The redundant Nant-y-Gro dam in mid-Wales was earmarked for explosives trials. This is a scale model of the dam, built to test calculations. (TRL Ltd)

Special measuring equipment was used to gauge the efficacy of the scaled-down explosive charges used against the dam wall. (TRL Ltd)

In April 1942 Wallis hit upon the idea of a bouncing bomb that could be dropped from an aircraft and skipped across the surface of a dam's reservoir, in much the same way as a flat pebble can be made to skim over the surface of water, except that in his idea for the bomb it rotated around a horizontal axis. He began work on a proposal for a spherical bomb that could be mechanically spun by the launching aircraft and released from very low level over the dam reservoir. It would then bounce across the surface of the water until it made contact with the dam wall. As it

An explosive charge is detonated against the inside wall of the real Nant-y-Gro dam.
(TRL Ltd)

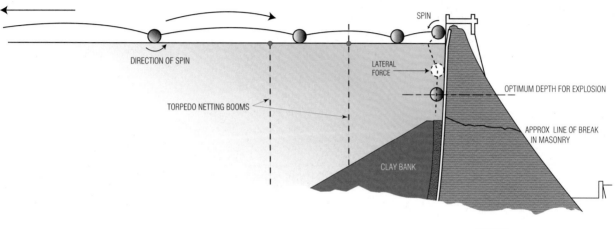

POINT OF RELEASE - APPROX 400-450 YDS UPSTREAM

DIRECTION OF SPIN

SPIN

LATERAL FORCE

OPTIMUM DEPTH FOR EXPLOSION

TORPEDO NETTING BOOMS

APPROX LINE OF BREAK IN MASONRY

CLAY BANK

ROCK BED

◄
The 640ft-long No. 2 Ship Tank at the National Physical Laboratory, Teddington, used by Wallis to perfect the delivery of the spherical weapon that eventually became the cylindrical bouncing bomb, codenamed 'Upkeep'. (HMSO National Physical Laboratory)

▲
How Barnes Wallis's revolutionary bouncing bomb was designed to bounce across the surface of the water, skipping over anti-torpedo nets before striking the inner face of the dam wall and sliding beneath the water to a predetermined depth, then exploding and breaching the structure. (Bow Watkinson)

sank to a predetermined depth, hydrostatic pistols inside the bomb would detonate the main explosive charge against the inner wall of the dam. Water pressure would do the rest.

In June, trials of the bouncing bomb concept using spheres the size of cricket balls were carried out in the 640ft-long water-filled ship tank at the National Physical Laboratory in Teddington. The top brass from the Air

A Wellington releases a spherical mine off Chesil Beach in Dorset. (IWM)

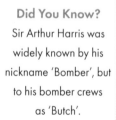

Did You Know?

Sir Arthur Harris was widely known by his nickname 'Bomber', but to his bomber crews as 'Butch'.

Ministry and MAP who came to observe were so impressed that they gave the go-ahead for full-scale live trials.

On 3 December 1942 a Wellington bomber made the first test-drop of a full-size mine off Chesil Beach in Dorset. Initial results were not good because the mines shattered when they hit the water, but further test-drops refined the design and the bouncing bomb finally proved itself on 5 February 1943. It was not until late in April that the size and shape of the weapon was finally decided upon.

Did You Know?
'Peter' Portal originally joined the Royal Engineers in 1914 as a private soldier. He was later commissioned and transferred to the Royal Flying Corps as an observer.

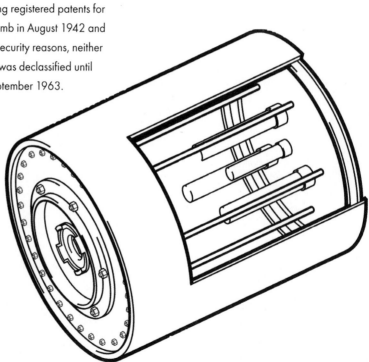

A cutaway drawing of the bouncing bomb, showing the three hydrostatic pistols and the shorter single self-destruct pistol (centre). (Paul Couper)

*'As I always thought – the weapon is balmy [*sic*]. I will not have aircraft flying about with spotlights on in a defended area. Get some of these lunatics controlled and if possible locked up!'*
'Bomber' Harris

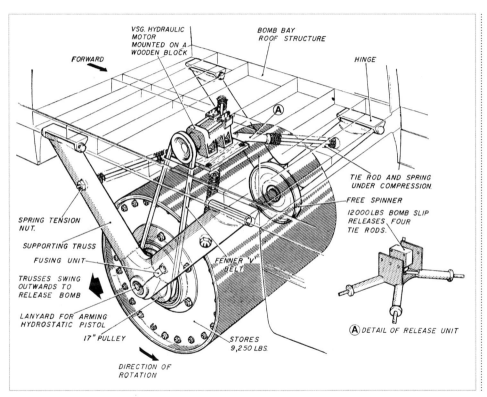

VSG. HYDRAULIC MOTOR MOUNTED ON A WOODEN BLOCK

BOMB BAY ROOF STRUCTURE

FORWARD

HINGE

A

TIE ROD AND SPRING UNDER COMPRESSION.

FREE SPINNER

12000LBS BOMB SLIP RELEASES FOUR TIE RODS.

SPRING TENSION NUT.

SUPPORTING TRUSS

FUSING UNIT

FENNER 'V' BELT

TRUSSES SWING OUTWARDS TO RELEASE BOMB

LANYARD FOR ARMING HYDROSTATIC PISTOL

17" PULLEY

STORES 9,250 LBS.

DIRECTION OF ROTATION

(A) DETAIL OF RELEASE UNIT

◄

The bouncing bomb installation as fitted to the modified Avro Lancaster BIII (Type 464 Provisioning).

Did You Know?
Upkeep is most accurately described as a revolving depth charge, but contemporary British documents refer to it as a mine. Since then it has been more generally described as a bouncing bomb.

Continued resistance to the idea from the MAP, Air Chief Marshal Sir Arthur 'Bomber' Harris, Commander-in-Chief, RAF Bomber Command, and Lord Cherwell (Frederick Lindemann, Churchill's personal scientific adviser) nearly put paid to the weapon, but the timely intervention of Sir Charles Portal, Chief of the Air Staff, saved the day. He overruled their concerns and ordered that the project should go ahead with the utmost urgency. Further orders were issued for the immediate conversion of three Lancaster bombers for operational trials, a further twenty for operational use, and the manufacture of 150 bouncing bombs.

Codenamed 'Upkeep' by the RAF, Wallis's bouncing bomb is more accurately described as a cylindrical air-dropped mine. It contained 6,600lb of Torpex explosive, which was detonated by three hydrostatic pistols at a depth of 30ft. The whole bomb weighed in at 9,250lb (or 4.12 tons) and was carried by a specially modified Avro Lancaster.

Slung beneath the belly of the Lancaster, the bomb was mounted between two side-swing calliper arms. The power to spin the cylindrical bomb before its release was transferred via a belt-drive from a small Vickers-Jassey variable-gear hydraulic motor that was mounted in the floor of the fuselage, and attached to one side of the weapon.

Back-spun at 500rpm, Upkeep needed to be dropped on to the reservoir by a Lancaster flying at 210mph from a height of 60ft at a distance of some 1,200–1,500ft from the dam face. To enable the Lancasters to fly at the required height to release the bomb, twin spotlights were fitted into the undersides of the aircraft and set to converge on the surface of the water at a height of 60ft. When the bomb aimer pressed the bomb-release button, powerful springs caused the calliper arms to spring outwards, allowing the bomb to drop free from the aircraft. Skipping over protective anti-torpedo nets it would bounce across the surface of the water towards the dam.

Wallis had worked out how to destroy a dam, but the problems he now faced were threefold: how to carry a big enough explosive charge to the target, how to drop it accurately, and then how to ensure that it was placed up against the inner dam wall when it exploded.

◄

To be effective, Upkeep needed to be dropped from a height of 60ft. In this scene from The Dam Busters *film, Guy Gibson opens the attack on the Möhne dam.*
(Canal Plus screengrab)

Lhe Avro Lancaster was the third, and most successful, of the RAF's trio of four-engine heavy bombers to enter service in the Second World War. It flew its first operation on 3/4 March 1942 and by April 1943 the Lancaster dominated Bomber Command's frontline strength, when seventeen squadrons were equipped with the type.

In 1943 the Lancaster was the only bomber aircraft in the RAF's inventory that was capable of carrying the 4-ton weapon envisaged by Barnes Wallis, as well as being

Did You Know?

In addition to its superlative weight-lifting capabilities, the Lancaster was also chosen to carry Upkeep because its bomb bay yielded more readily to the extensive modifications required than that of the Stirling or Halifax.

suitable for modification. In February, Avro was commissioned to build a prototype of what was cryptically referred to as the 'Type 464 Provisioning' Lancaster, a modified version of the standard Lancaster BIII adapted to carry the specially designed 'bouncing bomb'. Twenty-three of these Lancasters in the 'ED' serial range were ordered from Avro's Manchester factory.

To enable the top-secret new bomb to be carried, the Lancaster required certain modifications that altered its appearance substantially from the standard production Lancaster. The Frazer-Nash FN50 power-operated mid-upper turret, together with its associated equipment and ammunition, was removed and faired over; the twin bomb doors that ran almost the length of the fuselage underside, together with the internal bomb racks and associated equipment,

◀◀
The Avro Lancaster was arguably the finest heavy bomber of the Second World War. These Lancaster Mk Is are of 44 Squadron, the first RAF unit to be equipped with the type. (IWM TR206)

18

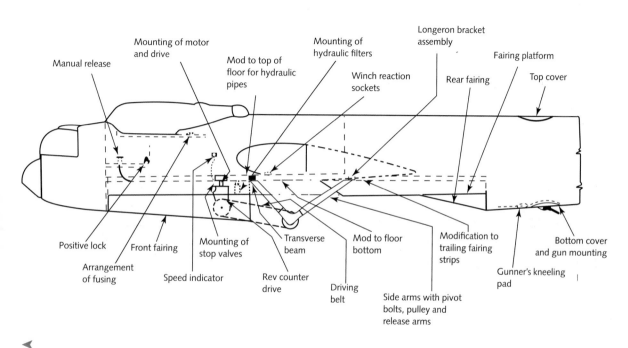

Manual release

Mounting of motor
and drive

Mod to top of
floor for hydraulic
pipes

Mounting of
hydraulic filters

Longeron bracket
assembly

Fairing platform

Winch reaction
sockets

Rear fairing

Top cover

Positive lock

Front fairing

Mounting of
stop valves

Transverse
beam

Mod to floor
bottom

Modification to
trailing fairing
strips

Bottom cover
and gun mounting

Arrangement
of fusing

Speed indicator

Rev counter
drive

Driving
belt

Side arms with pivot
bolts, pulley and
release arms

Gunner's kneeling
pad

Lancaster ED817/G, AJ-C, shows the cutaway bomb bay
and absence of dorsal turret that characterised the 'dam
buster' Lancasters. ED817 flew on the Upkeep dropping
trials at Reculver on 20 April 1943. (Bruce Robertson collection)

This drawing shows the modifications made to the
standard Avro Lancaster design to convert it to the
Type 464 Provisioning configuration. (Author's collection)

20

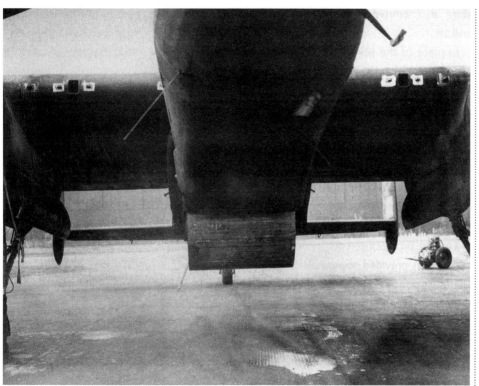

In this view from beneath the Lancaster's nose, looking aft, the Upkeep weapon can be seen protruding from the converted bomb bay.
(Crown Copyright)

This view of ED825/G, AJ-T, shows the side-swing callipers and drive belt beneath the fuselage. Flt Lt Joe McCarthy flew ED825 on the dams raid.
(IWM ATP 11384B)

were also removed and faired over fore and aft.

In place of the bomb bay, a recess was created in which the bouncing bomb was held between a pair of side-swing, V-shaped calliper arms, each fitted with a 20in-diameter disc. These discs corresponded to two circular tracks, one at each end of the cylindrical bomb. Back-spin was transmitted to the bomb by friction generated between the driven discs and the circular tracks. The Vickers-Jassey motor, driving a belt running in a groove on the driven disc in the starboard calliper arm, provided power for the rotation. Hydraulic power originally used by the mid-upper turret and bomb bay doors was diverted to the hydraulic motor in the floor of the fuselage.

Despite the removal of the mid-upper turret and bomb doors, there was no saving in tare weight. In fact, the additional equipment fitted resulted in a weight increase of approximately 1,190lb (540kg).

Avro and Vickers jointly undertook modification of the Lancasters, with the latter using facilities at RAE Farnborough. Such was the urgency of the task that both contractors worked round-the-clock shifts, seven days a week.

Because of the great haste in which the contractors had been asked to carry out the modifications, not everything was completed

'. . . [the Lancaster] was the only aircraft in the world capable of doing the job, and I should like to pay my tribute of congratulations and admiration to you, the designer.'
Barnes Wallis to Roy Chadwick, 25 May 1943

on time to meet the Air Ministry's tight deadline. Therefore some of the work on the Lancasters that should have been undertaken by Avro was carried out at Scampton by the base engineering staff, jointly assisted by supervisors from Avro, RAE Farnborough and the Ministry of Aircraft Production.

It was not until 8 April that the first of the modified Type 464 Provisioning Lancasters reached the squadron. By the end of the month, thirteen had arrived and, by early May, eighteen. The full complement of nineteen aircraft was reached by 14 May – two days before the raid.

▲
A well-known photograph of Wg Cdr Guy Gibson's Lancaster, ED932/G, AJ-G, showing the cutaway bomb bay, the Upkeep weapon mounted between the side-swing callipers, and the belt drive to the weapon. (Crown Copyright)

23

On 15 March 1943 'Bomber' Harris ordered the formation of a special new bomber squadron. The Commander-in-Chief's change of heart was due largely to pressure from the Chief of the Air Staff, Sir Charles Portal, who had been impressed by the bomb trials at Chesil Beach and the model tests in the ship tank at Teddington. Portal now wanted development of the bomb, modification of the aircraft and training of the Lancaster crews to proceed with the utmost urgency if the attack on the dams was to be mounted before the latest optimum date of 26 May.

The new squadron was officially formed on 17 March and known initially as 'Squadron X'. It was to be commanded by a highly experienced, 24-year-old wing commander named Guy Gibson, with one night fighter and two bomber tours already to his credit.

Bomber Command decreed that the crews for this new squadron were to be volunteers who had already completed at least one, and possibly two, bomber tours. Contrary to popular myth, not all the pilots were personally known to Gibson. The majority

'Guy Gibson did not personally select the pilots and crews. All squadrons in 5 Group were circulated, calling for volunteer crews nearing the end of their first tour or commencing their second, to join a new squadron being formed for a special operation. David Maltby, Joe McCarthy and I were all on 97 Squadron at the time and volunteered. We were not arbitrarily posted.'

Flt Lt Les Munro, captain, AJ-W

◄◄
Wg Cdr Guy Gibson (centre) was posted to Scampton from 106 Squadron to command the secret new squadron, known initially as 'Squadron X'.
(Crown Copyright)

were not decorated and some had yet to complete their first operational tour. Many of the aircrew had completed fewer than ten operations against enemy targets, and some were actually on their first.

No. 106 Squadron provided three crew captains in Flt Lt John Hopgood, Flt Lt David Shannon DFC, RAAF, and Flt Sgt Lewis Burpee DFM, RCAF. Another 5 Group squadron, No. 57, provided three more pilots in the shape of Plt Off Geoff Rice, Flt Lt Bill Astell DFC, and Sqn Ldr Melvin 'Dinghy' Young DFC. 'Dinghy' was so named because he had ditched twice in the North Sea. Young was Gibson's deputy as well as the commander of A Flight.

The B Flight commander was ex-50 Squadron Sqn Ldr Henry Maudslay DFC. Also from 50 Squadron were Flt Lt Mick Martin DFC (a highly experienced Aussie pilot serving in the RAF, and an expert in low-level flying) and Plt Off Les Knight RAAF. In fact, 50 Squadron had been the breeding ground for some of the finest pilots and crews in Bomber Command, of which Guy Gibson and Mick Martin were among the three greatest bomber pilots of the Second World War.

No. 207 Squadron provided Plt Off Warner Ottley DFC, while 44 Squadron supplied Flt Sgt Ken Brown RCAF and Plt Off Vernon Byers RCAF.

From left to right: Flt Lt David Shannon (captain, AJ-L), Flt Lt Dick Trevor-Roper (rear gunner in Gibson's crew) and Sqn Ldr George Holden, who was to succeed Gibson as the commanding officer of 617 Squadron soon after the dams raid. (IWM TR1129)

Did You Know?

Three pilots and their crews who were part of the original draft posted in to 617 Squadron in March 1943 did not fly on the dams raid. They were Flt Lt Harold and Plt Off William Divall, both of whose crews were prevented from flying on Chastise owing to sickness. Flt Sgt S.G. Lanchester RCAF and his crew opted to leave the squadron after Gibson threatened to replace their navigator.

From 97 Squadron came Flt Lt David Maltby DFC, Flt Lt Les Munro RNZAF, and an American, Flt Lt Joe McCarthy DFC, RCAF. From 61 Squadron came Flt Lt Robert Barlow DFC, RAAF, and from 49 Squadron Sgt Cyril Anderson and Sgt Bill Townsend DFM.

The 5 Group bomber airfield of Scampton, 5 miles north of the city of Lincoln, was chosen as the base for Squadron X. It was also home to another Lancaster squadron, No. 57. The new aircrews began to arrive at Scampton on 21 March and all non-flying personnel were on the base by 27 March. Squadron X officially became 617 Squadron on the 24th and was declared ready to fly on the 25th.

On the 24th, Gibson travelled to see Barnes Wallis at Weybridge, where the scientist outlined his ideas on the bomb and showed him a film of the recent trials at Chesil Beach.

◄

The two New Zealanders on 617 were Flg Off L. Chambers (wireless operator in Flt Lt Mick Martin's crew) and Flt Lt Les Munro, captain of AJ-W. (IWM CH9937)

◄◄

Plt Off Les Knight RAAF (AJ-N) and his crew. From left to right: Hobday, Johnson, Sutherland, Knight, Kellow, Grayston and O'Brien. (IWM CH11049)

Flt Lt Joe McCarthy and crew (AJ-T). From left to right: Johnson, McLean, Batson, McCarthy, Radcliffe, Eaton. Missing from this photograph is Flg Off D. Rodger, the rear gunner. (IWM TR1128)

Flt Lt David Maltby (captain of AJ-J, seen here after the dams raid as a squadron leader) and Wg Cdr Guy Gibson, in the latter's office at Scampton. (IWM TR1122)

31

On the 27th, Gibson was given orders that outlined why the new squadron had been formed. Specific details of their intended target were still withheld, but he was told how 617 Squadron would be required to attack a number of lightly defended special targets, necessitating low-level navigation over enemy territory in moonlight with a final approach to the target at 100ft and a precise speed of 240mph. Gibson was advised to ensure that his crews practised low-level flying over water, and on daylight training sorties to ensure that pilots and bomb aimers wore dark goggles to simulate moonlight

Did You Know?

The mix of aircrews on 617 Squadron was truly international, with 90 men from the RAF, 29 RCAF, 12 RAAF and 2 RNZAF.

◀◀

RAF Scampton and its environs. The close proximity of airfields in eastern England at this time of the war often meant that their flying circuit patterns overlapped. (Crown Copyright)

◀

Squadron X became 617 Squadron on 24 March 1943. (Crown Copyright)

Did You Know?

To simulate night-flying conditions during daylight, blue celluloid was applied to the cockpit canopy and the gunners' turret Perspex, and amber-tinted interchangeable lenses were fitted to flying goggles.

conditions. Gibson was also told that there were nine lakes in Wales and the Midlands suitable for flying practice. No. 617 Squadron was now ready to begin its intensive flying training programme using ten 'borrowed' standard Lancasters.

On the 28th, Gibson, Flt Lt John Hopgood and Sqn Ldr Melvin 'Dinghy' Young practised low flying in Lancasters over the Derwent reservoir and dam in the Peak District. During

daylight Gibson found this a relatively easy task, but when he attempted to do the same at dusk it became clear just how dangerous the job was going to be.

The next day Gibson visited 5 Group HQ, where he was shown scale models of the Möhne and Sorpe dams and told to visit Wallis again. On his next visit to Weybridge, the construction of the Ruhr dams and their importance to German heavy industry were explained to Gibson.

Photoreconnaissance of the dams was undertaken by Spitfires of the RAF's PR

It was vital for 617's crews to be able to fly safely over water by night, at low level. Here again is the BBMF's Lancaster, pictured over the English Channel. (Richard Winslade)

squadrons. Over the coming weeks they would provide vital information to Bomber Command's planning staff about water levels in the dams' reservoirs and intelligence on anti-aircraft defences in the vicinity.

Two important technical matters could still make or break all their hard work – an effective bombsight with which to aim the bombs accurately, and a means of precisely calculating the height of an aircraft above the reservoirs.

First, the extreme low level at which the bombs were to be dropped meant that no bombsight then in use by the RAF could do the job. Surprisingly, the solution was very simple and effective. A hand-held wooden sight, designed by Wg Cdr C.L. Dann at the A&AEE Boscombe Down, achieved an accurate release point for the Upkeep weapon. Dann used calculations based on the width between the sluice towers of the Möhne dam to make a simple triangular wooden sight. With a sighting peephole at the apex and two nails at the extremities of the base, the bomb aimer held the sight by a wooden handle attached to the underside of the apex and looked through the peephole. On the bombing run, when the twin towers of the dam coincided with the two nails, the bomb aimer pressed the bomb release mechanism.

Some bomb aimers dispensed with the Dann sight altogether and experimented with their own sighting devices, which included chinagraph pencil marks on the clear-vision Perspex panel in the bomb-aiming position, and lengths of string attached to screws each side of the panel to create a large triangle.

Second, was the conundrum of how to maintain a specific height at low level over water and in the dark. Ben Lockspeiser, civilian Director of Scientific Research at MAP, solved it. Trials were carried out using twin spotlights fitted to an aircraft; these converged on the surface of the water. After a series of tests, it was decided that the optimum positioning for the twin Aldis lamps on a Lancaster would be one in the port side of the nose, aft of the bomb aimer's clear-vision panel, and the second in the rear of the bomb bay. Both lamps were angled to starboard and when the aircraft was flying at the prescribed 150ft (later reduced to 60ft) above the water, the twin beams would converge to form a figure of eight on the water beneath and just forward of the leading edge of the starboard wing. This enabled the navigator to check the height from the Perspex blister on the starboard side of the cockpit.

'The boys had begun to get good at their flying, and now I knew where and what the targets were we could plan a route similar to the one which would actually be used over Germany. This meant flying a lot over lakes, but the excuse was always the same: they were good landmarks and a good check on navigation. As we would have to fly to Germany at tree-level height, keeping to track was most important, and it meant navigation to the yard'.

Wg Cdr Guy Gibson

Throughout April, when weather conditions permitted, the crews of 617 Squadron carried out intensive flying training on a daily basis, and by the end of that month Gibson was able to report that all his crews could

Flt Lt Joe McCarthy nearly missed his chance to take part in the operation when his own Lancaster went unserviceable at the last minute. This is ED825/G, the Lancaster actually flown by McCarthy on the raid.
(Crown Copyright)

navigate at low level by night, fly safely over water at a height of 150ft and bomb accurately with the aid of a special bombsight.

By the end of April, thirteen Type 464 Provisioning aircraft had arrived on the squadron, which meant that the borrowed unmodified Lancasters, used until then for training purposes, could be returned to their owner squadrons. By early May, eighteen modified Lancasters had been received and fitted with VHF radios; twenty Upkeep

◄

The first modified Lancasters arrived at Scampton in April. ED817/G took part in the Upkeep dropping trials at Reculver on 20 April, but did not fly on the actual dams raid.
(Bruce Robertson collection)

➤➤
*Lake Bala in North Wales
was one of several lakes
used by 617 to practise
night flying at low level.*
(Author)

weapons had also been received and were ready for balancing (to ensure they rotated true and did not oscillate); practice Upkeeps had been delivered and were being prepared for crews to use in a night trial off Reculver on the north Kent coast.

From 5 May, all training was undertaken at the Eyebrook reservoir in Rutland, where ten Lancasters at a time practised flying at 60ft above the water. Abberton reservoir near Colchester and Lake Bala in North Wales were also used for low-level flying and bombing practice. In the days that followed, the skills of 617's bomber crews were honed to a high degree of operational capability: pilots could fly at 60ft over water while maintaining an airspeed of 210mph; using 'Gee' and with careful map reading, navigators could find their way around the countryside with precision at low level in the dark; bomb aimers had refined their techniques with practice bombs to achieve an average error of 117ft (35.7m); and gunners had sharpened their gunnery skills to make them potent adversaries for enemy night fighters and flak gunners.

On the night of 6/7 May, the squadron flew a full exercise over the Eyebrook, Abberton and Howden reservoirs, Derwent dam, Wainfleet and the Wash, simulating the attack pattern that had been planned for the actual operation. The rest of the squadron practised bombing over the Wash with the aid of their twin Aldis spotlights.

On 10 May Scampton's station commander, Gp Capt Charles Whitworth, was given a draft order for the forthcoming operation. The attack was to be mounted by twenty Lancasters, with three sections of three aircraft taking off at 10-minute

intervals, followed by individual aircraft taking off at 3-minute intervals. Aircraft were to cross the North Sea at 60ft and maintain this low level across the Continent, with the formation leader climbing to 500ft en route to check landmarks and, when 10 miles from the target, climbing to between 1,000 and 1,500ft. Targets were designated A, B and C, corresponding to the Möhne, Eder and Sorpe dams. The leader would make an immediate

> A modified Lancaster drops a full-size Upkeep in the sea on the north Kent coast at Reculver Bay, near Margate, in May 1943. (IWM FLM2340)

>> An inert Upkeep filled with concrete bowls up the beach at Reculver. A small group of intrepid observers, including Gibson and Wallis, looks on. (IWM FLM2343)

43

➤➤
*This remarkable
sequence of movie stills
taken in May 1943 shows
a modified Lancaster
making a trial drop of an
Upkeep weapon. In the
fourth photograph, the
tailplane appears to have
been damaged by the
great plume of water
made by the bomb on its
first bounce.*
(IWM FLM2360/1/2/3)

assault on target A and, when he had completed his attack, he would wait 90 seconds before calling in the second aircraft to attack, followed by the third. By this time the second formation would have arrived and the procedure would be repeated, with the third formation following on. Each aircraft would fire a red flare over the dam after dropping its mine as a safety precaution for the next aircraft in line to attack. When target A had been destroyed, aircraft would divert to B, where they would follow the same attack pattern, while simultaneously target C would be attacked by five Lancasters as a distraction from the attacks under way on targets A and B. After completing their attacks, individual crews were to make their own way home at low level and high speed.

During April and early May, a series of trial weapon drops using spheres were made in the sea off Reculver. As a test area it offered better security than Chesil Beach in Dorset, and it also allowed easier recovery of the dropped weapons for examination. From their results, the final shape and size of the bouncing bomb were determined as a cylinder and not a sphere. Among the trial

'[When] we carried out another dress rehearsal . . . six out of the twelve aircraft were very seriously damaged by the great columns of water sent up when their mines splashed in. They had been flying slightly too low. Most of the damage was around the tails of the aircraft; elevators were smashed like plywood, turrets were knocked in, fins were bent. It was a miracle some of them got home.'

Wg Cdr Guy Gibson

observers was Barnes Wallis, accompanied by Guy Gibson.

On 1 May the first full-size Upkeep cylinder was dropped at Reculver. On the 11th, three of the new Type 464 Provisioning Lancasters of 617 Squadron dropped inert Upkeeps at Reculver for the first time, and the next day further aircraft from the squadron carried out more trial drops. These practice attacks continued for the next two

► *Wg Cdr Guy Gibson pilots his Lancaster over the Reculver range on 11 May, having just released his Upkeep weapon.* (IWM FLM2353)

days, but two precious aircraft were damaged in the process, one beyond repair. On the 13th, the only fully armed live Upkeep mine to be spun and dropped before the operation was released from a Lancaster in a trial 5 miles off the Kent coast at Broadstairs.

On the evening of the 14th, nineteen specially modified Type 464 Provisioning Lancasters flew their last exercise together before Operation Chastise. The following day, last-minute checks and adjustments were made to the weapon and its release mechanism after a second live Upkeep was dropped off Broadstairs, but this time without being spun.

The stage was now set for the big 'op'.

▼ *Gibson's black Labrador dog, Nigger, was run over and killed by a car outside the camp gate at Scampton the day before Operation Chastise was due to take place. His death was not widely publicised on the station, in case it was seen as a bad omen by the aircrews of 617 Squadron.* (Bruce Robertson collection)

Photoreconnaissance (or PR) was vital to the success of Operation Chastise. It provided important information to Bomber Command's planners about when the water levels in the reservoirs behind the dams had reached their maximum flood damage potential. When full, the Möhne reservoir contained some 140 million tons of water and was the principal source of supply for the industries of the Ruhr valley 20 miles away. PR also gave important up-to-date intelligence on whether anti-aircraft defences had been strengthened on the dams themselves and in the surrounding countryside.

On 25 January 1943 orders were issued from Bomber Command Headquarters to the RAF's PR squadrons stationed at RAF Benson in Oxfordshire, to obtain photographic coverage of the Möhne dam and its reservoir. It was not until 7 February that the first of a series of nine PR sorties was flown by Supermarine Spitfires of 541 Squadron from Benson.

In December 1942 the Spitfire PR XI had entered service with 541 Squadron. It represented a quantum leap in speed and altitude performance over previous PR marks. The PR XI was completely unarmed and had been modified from the standard Spitfire Mk IX to carry extra fuel in wing leading-edge tanks to increase its range, as well as incorporating an enlarged oil tank beneath the nose. It also featured a fully retractable tail wheel. The PR XI was the first reconnaissance version of the Spitfire to go into production with the 1,565hp Rolls-Royce Merlin 61 engine, driving a four-blade propeller, which gave a service ceiling of 44,000ft and a cruising speed of 397mph at 31,000ft. When fitted with a 170-gallon overload fuel tank, carried

Did You Know?
PR Spitfires were fitted with special wings to carry extra fuel. They took a third more man-hours to build than a standard Spitfire fighter.

◄◄
This photograph of the Möhne dam was taken on 3 April 1943 from a Spitfire PR XI of 541 Squadron, flown by Flg Off J.R. Brew. (Crown Copyright)

RAF photo-reconnaissance aircraft in 1943 were painted overall in cerulean blue, a deep shade which became known as 'PR blue'.

➤➤
From January 1943, Supermarine Spitfire PR IX and XI aircraft were used to reconnoitre the Ruhr dams. This is a PR XI. Note the oblique camera port to the left of the fuselage roundel. Two vertical cameras were carried in the belly of the aircraft, just below the roundel. (Peter R. March)

beneath the belly, the aircraft was blessed with a range of some 2,300 miles, which made it capable of ranging far and wide across occupied Europe.

The business end of the aircraft was in the underside of the rear fuselage where a split pair of vertical cameras, either F24 or F52, were installed. A choice of lenses enabled high-resolution photographs to be taken of ground targets from heights of up to 40,000ft. An oblique F24 camera could also be fitted in the port side of the fuselage above the vertical camera installations.

The PR XI's exemplary performance at high altitude gave it near immunity from interception by enemy fighters for nearly a year, until the appearance of the first German jet fighters in the summer of 1944. From 1943, the blue-painted PR XI was the most numerous photo-reconnaissance variant in

'The most important operational requirement for survival on PR operations throughout the war was the ability of the pilot to keep a really effective lookout for enemy activity during the whole course of a sortie. No matter how good his aircraft, if the enemy saw him first the pilot was a sitting duck.'

Flt Lt Freddie Ball, reconnaissance pilot,
1 PRU and 540 Squadron

use with the RAF, with 471 examples built.

During February, the weather conditions experienced over western Germany were not kind to the 'recce' pilots. It took seven attempts to photograph the Möhne before anything useful for intelligence purposes was finally obtained from the sortie flown on 19 February. It took two further sorties, with

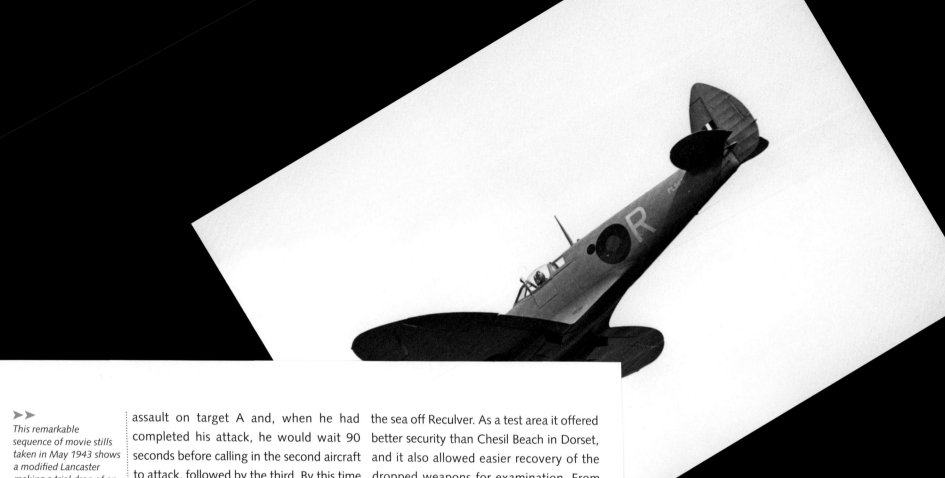

assault on target A and, when he had completed his attack, he would wait 90 seconds before calling in the second aircraft to attack, followed by the third. By this time the second formation would have arrived and the procedure would be repeated, with the third formation following on. Each aircraft would fire a red flare over the dam after dropping its mine as a safety precaution for the next aircraft in line to attack. When target A had been destroyed, aircraft would divert to B, where they would follow the same attack pattern, while simultaneously target C would be attacked by five Lancasters as a distraction from the attacks under way on targets A and B. After completing their attacks, individual crews were to make their own way home at low level and high speed.

During April and early May, a series of trial weapon drops using spheres were made in the sea off Reculver. As a test area it offered better security than Chesil Beach in Dorset, and it also allowed easier recovery of the dropped weapons for examination. From their results, the final shape and size of the bouncing bomb were determined as a cylinder and not a sphere. Among the trial

'[When] we carried out another dress rehearsal . . . six out of the twelve aircraft were very seriously damaged by the great columns of water sent up when their mines splashed in. They had been flying slightly too low. Most of the damage was around the tails of the aircraft; elevators were smashed like plywood, turrets were knocked in, fins were bent. It was a miracle some of them got home.'

Wg Cdr Guy Gibson

Did You Know?

The F52 camera, introduced in January 1942, was an enlarged version of the F24 for high-altitude day photo-reconnaissance work. The film format was increased in size from 5in square to 8¼ x 7in, with a choice of lenses offering focal lengths of 14in, 20in or 36in. The film magazine capacity was 250 or 500 exposures.

the last completed on 4 April, to provide photographs of sufficient quality for the Model Section at the Central Interpretation Unit (CIU), RAF Medmenham. Their task was to build a scale model of the Möhne dam and

surrounding landscape with which to brief Gibson and his Lancaster crews when the time came. Periodically, in the weeks that followed, 541 and 542 Squadrons photographed the dam to provide additional information about the dam itself and changes in the water level and defences.

It was generally the same pilots who, each time, flew the PR sorties over the Ruhr dams. The intention was that they would get to know the dams and their hinterland so well that when they over flew them in post-raid reconnaissance sorties they would be more likely to notice changes in the landscape made by the floodwaters and report them at their debriefing. Just in case the enemy got wind of the impending operation, the RAF's PR pilots were briefed to cover a variety of targets in the Ruhr valley and across Holland in the same sortie so as not to draw undue attention to their real interest.

In early April, Bomber Command made a further request for photographic coverage, only this time of the Eder and Sorpe dams, which lay some 50 miles south-east and 6 miles south-west respectively of the

One of the PRU's objectives was to bring back high-quality photographs to help skilled model makers build three-dimensional scale models of the dams. This is a model of the Sorpe dam. (IWM MH3780)

These models were of great importance for aircrew briefing purposes. This is the Möhne dam. (IWM MH842)

Möhne. The Eder was even bigger than the Möhne, containing more than 200 million tons of water, although its use was primarily for water management purposes and not to feed industry in the Ruhr. Spitfire PR XIs of 542 Squadron completed the reconnaissance on 15 May. By mid-afternoon the same day,

'A PR pilot was always vulnerable during long photographic runs, when he was concentrating on accuracy over the target and did not see a fighter or flak until it was too late.'

Flt Lt Freddie Ball, reconnaissance pilot, 1 PRU and 540 Squadron

➤
A scale model of the Eder dam. (IWM MH27710)

the results of these recce flights and the all-important intelligence interpretations were ready. The skilled model makers at CIU Medmenham made their final changes to the detailed scale models of the dams and the surrounding landscape, for use at the aircrew briefing the following day. Meanwhile, Benson and its PR Spitfire pilots stood by to photograph the results of the raid, now only a day away.

◀
This incredible mosaic of the Möhne dam, its lake and hinterland was made up from dozens of photoreconnaissance photographs.
(Crown Copyright)

Wg Cdr Guy Gibson led the first wave of nine aircraft to take off. (IWM CH11047)

After months of guesswork, the crews were finally notified of their targets in the main briefings at Scampton on the afternoon of 16 May. Their 'favourite' had been a precision attack on the battleship *Tirpitz*; but the reality was six huge dams in western Germany, located to the east and south-east of the Ruhr valley.

Nineteen Lancasters were to fly in three waves, the first comprising nine aircraft in three sections led by Wg Cdr Guy Gibson, their target the Möhne dam. The first wave consisted of Gibson, Hopgood, Martin, Young, Astell, Maltby, Maudslay, Knight and Shannon. They were to fly the southern route from Scampton, across the North Sea to the Scheldt estuary, making landfall between Noord Beveland and Schouwen, and thence to the Möhne dam, where they were to press home their attack. If the Möhne was successfully breached, any aircraft whose mines had not been dropped were to fly on to attack the Eder dam.

The second wave of five Lancasters, led by Flt Lt Joe McCarthy, an American, and comprising Byers, Barlow, Rice and Munro, was to bomb the Sorpe dam. They were

Operation Chastise gets under way. An unidentified Lancaster of 617 Squadron takes off from Scampton's grass runway and heads for Germany on 16 May. (IWM CH18006)

actually to take off first and fly singly by way of a more northerly route across the North Sea to the Dutch island of Vlieland, before heading inland to join the same route to the Möhne dam as the first wave.

A third, reserve, wave of five Lancasters led by Plt Off Warner Ottley, consisting of Townsend, Anderson, Brown and Burpee, was to take off two hours later and fly the same southerly route as the first wave, to attack the last-resort targets – the Diemel, Ennepe and Lister dams. But if the three main target dams had not been breached, they would be called upon to attack them.

Low-level flying was essential at all times to avoid being picked up by German radar, and attracting the unwelcome attention of flak and night fighters. Shortly before 2130 hr on the evening of 16 May 1943, the first of nineteen Lancasters took off from Scampton,

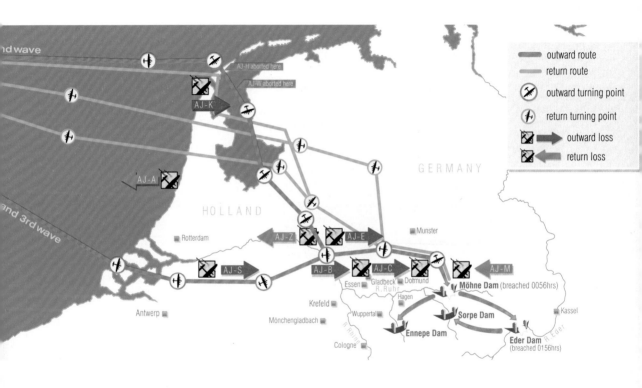

outward route
return route
outward turning point
return turning point
outward loss
return loss

GERMANY

AJ-H aborted here
AJ-W aborted here

AJ-K

AJ-A

HOLLAND

AJ-Z

AJ-E

Munster

Rotterdam

AJ-S

AJ-B

AJ-C

AJ-M

Essen

Gladbeck

Dotmund

Möhne Dam (breached 0056hrs)

R. Ruhr

Krefeld

Hagen

Antwerp

Wuppertal

Sorpe Dam

Kassel

Mönchengladbach

R. Ruhr

Ennepe Dam

Eder Dam
(breached 0156hrs)

R. Eder

Cologne

nd wave

and 3rd wave

59

each carrying a bouncing bomb beneath its belly. They headed at low level across the North Sea and crossed the Dutch coast, before making their way inland across Holland and Germany, at between 60 and 100ft, towards the Ruhr valley. Plt Off Geoff Rice had to return to base early after his Lancaster, AJ-H, struck the sea in a glancing blow that ripped off its bomb. The third flight had suffered the first fatality of the night when Lancaster AJ-B, piloted by Flt Lt Bill Astell, flew into an electricity pylon en route across Germany, and exploded, killing all on board.

Four more aircraft were shot down by flak or crashed on the way to the target – Plt Off Vernon Byers in AJ-K, Plt Off Lewis Burpee in AJ-S, Flt Lt Bob Barlow in AJ-E and Plt Off Warner Ottley in AJ-C. Flt Lt Les Munro's Lancaster, AJ-W, was badly holed by flak that caused it to turn for home without bombing.

'We were flying at 240mph and I would have been at 70 or 60 feet when we were hit over Vlieland on the port side of the aircraft. The intercom immediately went dead. I felt the thump of the shell. The damage from the shell exploding blew a hole in the side of the aircraft where the squadron codes were.'

Flt Lt Les Munro, captain, AJ-W

Out of an initial force of nineteen aircraft, this left twelve Lancasters to bomb the dams. The first flight, led by Gibson, arrived over the Möhne dam at 0020 hr, followed minutes afterwards by the second and third flights.

Amid intense flak, Gibson opened the attack on the Möhne, releasing his mine from a height of 60ft while flying his Lancaster at a speed of 240mph. The mine exploded but failed to breach the wall and it quickly became clear that the dam was going to be a tough nut to crack. Gibson drew the attention of the defending flak gunners while four

Pausing to speak to well wishers – possibly Air Vice-Marshal Cochrane, AOC 5 Group, and Gp Capt Whitworth, Scampton's station commander – Gibson and crew board their Lancaster. From left to right: Trevor-Roper, Pulford, Deering, Spafford, Hutchison, Gibson and Taerum.
(IWM CH18005)

Did You Know?

Flt Lt Joe McCarthy was forced to switch aircraft, from ED923/G to ED825/G, at the last minute because of an engine coolant leak. The replacement Lancaster was a reserve aircraft and fitted with neither VHF radio nor twin Aldis spotlights, but it had been bombed up and was ready to fly.

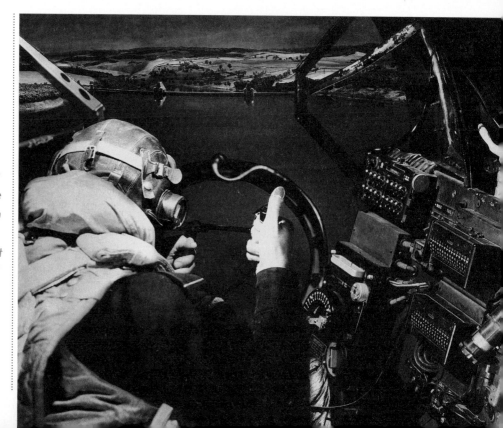

Gibson's bomb aimer, Flg Off Fred Spafford, released their Upkeep weapon, but it failed to breach the dam wall.
(Canal Plus E54.1.Prod.196)

'As we came over the hill we saw the Möhne lake. Then we saw the dam itself. In that light it looked squat and heavy and unconquerable.'

Wg Cdr Guy Gibson

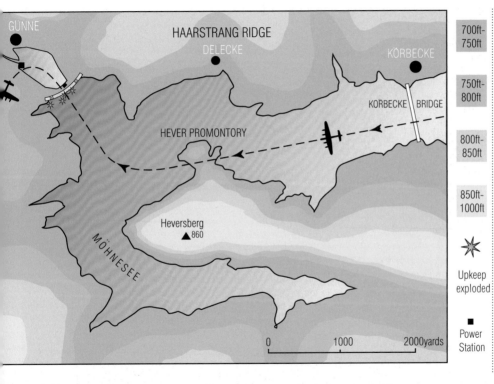

GÜNNE

HAARSTRANG RIDGE

DELECKE

KÖRBECKE

KÖRBECKE BRIDGE

HEVER PROMONTORY

MÖHNESEE

Heversberg
▲ 860

0   1000   2000yards

| 700ft-750ft |
| 750ft-800ft |
| 800ft-850ft |
| 850ft-1000ft |

✳ Upkeep exploded

■ Power Station

◀ *Map of the Möhne dam and its environs, showing the local topography and the direction of the attack.* (Bow Watkinson)

Did You Know?
Code words used on Operation Chastise:
Goner – special weapon released;
Nigger – target X breached (Möhne);
Dinghy – target Y breached (Eder).

In a scene from The Dam Busters *film, Guy Gibson, played by actor Richard Todd, looks on as the fictional Flt Lt David Maltby's Upkeep makes the vital breach in the Möhne dam at 0056 hr that caused the walls to burst.*
(Canal Plus E54.1.Prod.165)

The Möhne dam and its fast-emptying lake, photographed on 17 May by Flg Off Jerry Fray from his high-flying Spitfire PR XI. (IWM CH9687)

65

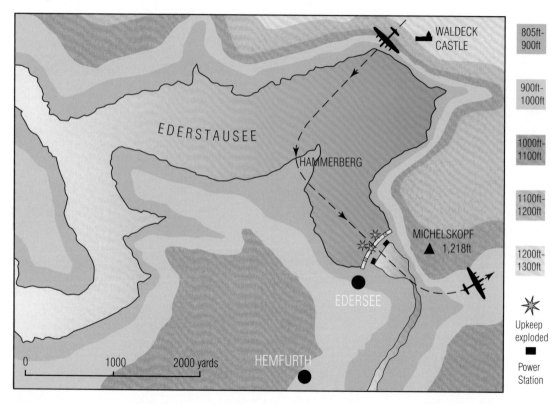

	805ft-900ft
	900ft-1000ft
	1000ft-1100ft
	1100ft-1200ft
	1200ft-1300ft

WALDECK CASTLE

EDERSTAUSEE

HAMMERBERG

MICHELSKOPF
▲ 1,218ft

EDERSEE

HEMFURTH

0   1000   2000 yards

✳ Upkeep exploded

■ Power Station

more crews, Flt Lt John Hopgood (AJ-M), Flt Lt Mick Martin (AJ-P), Sqn Ldr Melvyn Young (AJ-A), and Flt Lt David Maltby (AJ-J), bombed the Möhne dam in turn. On the fourth attempt they succeeded in breaching its walls. Maltby's aircraft (AJ-H) made the vital breach at 0056 hr that caused the dam to burst open.

Hopgood's Lancaster was hit by flak on its bomb run across the Möhne lake and its bouncing bomb overshot the parapet to explode below on the power house in the compensating basin. M for Mother struggled to gain height but crashed in flames on the hillside beyond the dam wall. Miraculously, two of her crew survived by baling out of the stricken bomber at low level.

Gibson then proceeded to fly 50 miles to bomb the Eder dam, accompanied by Flt Lt Dave Shannon (AJ-L), Sqn Ldr Henry Maudslay (AJ-Z) and Plt Off Les Knight (AJ-N), with Sqn Ldr Melvyn Young (AJ-A) as deputy leader. Unlike the Möhne and its hinterland, the Eder dam was undefended by flak guns or barrage balloons. However, owing to its geographical location in a steep, wooded valley, it proved more difficult to bomb than the Möhne. By the time the Lancasters arrived over the Eder lake, fog was beginning to form in the valley which made identification of the dam itself difficult. Shannon and Maudslay pressed home their attacks but without success and it was not until the tenth attempt that Les Knight's bomb spectacularly breached the Eder at 0154 hr.

Despite taking off 34 minutes late because of technical problems, Flt Lt Joe McCarthy (AJ-T) made up some time and arrived over the Sorpe dam at 0015 hr. He encountered

A pilot's-eye view of the Eder reservoir from Waldeck castle, looking down on to the Ederstausee, with the Hammerberg spit in the middle foreground. Beyond – half hidden by the forested promontory on the left – is the Eder dam itself. (Richard Simms)

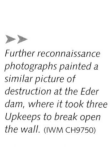

Further reconnaissance photographs painted a similar picture of destruction at the Eder dam, where it took three Upkeeps to break open the wall. (IWM CH9750)

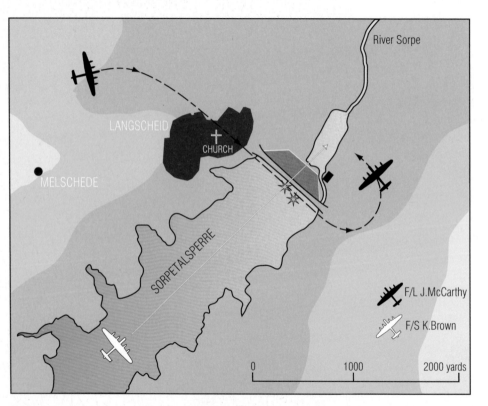

River Sorpe

LANGSCHEID

✝
CHURCH

● MELSCHEDE

SORPETALSPERRE

 F/L J.McCarthy

 F/S K.Brown

0	1000	2000 yards

928ft-1000ft

1000ft-1500ft

1500ft-2000ft

Earth Bank

✳ Upkeep exploded

 Power Station

the same problems with fog as Gibson and the other crews over the Eder. McCarthy's Lancaster was not fitted with the twin Aldis spotlights for accurate height-keeping, so it took him nine attempts flying along the crown of the dam wall before his bomb aimer released their bomb freefall at 0046 hr, without rotation. It failed to breach the dam but damaged the parapet.

Flt Sgt Ken Brown (AJ-F) reached the Sorpe dam some time later. He flew a head-on approach to the dam and on his tenth

SORPE DAM
(After attack)
K 1559
Neg. No. 24689

◄◄

Map of the Sorpe dam and its environs, showing the local topography and the direction of the attack. (Bow Watkinson)

►

The Sorpe dam remained unbreached, but its parapet structure had been damaged. Water spilled from the reservoir over the dam wall and into the compensating basin beneath.
(Crown Copyright)

Operation Chastise was costly for 617 Squadron. Eight Lancasters failed to return from the raid, and this meant the loss of 56 men – 53 killed, 3 prisoners-of-war. This is possibly the remains of 'Dinghy' Young's Lancaster, ED877/G, AJ-A, shot down when crossing the Dutch coast on its homeward journey from bombing the Möhne dam. All of the crew were killed.
(Crown Copyright)

run dropped his bomb, without rotation, at 0314 hr. It exploded against the dam wall, but the wall still held. Further damage had been done to the parapet, causing it to crumble, but the Sorpe dam remained largely intact and unbreached.

The eleventh Lancaster (AJ-Y), piloted by Flt Sgt Cyril Anderson, was unable to find its target of the Diemel dam and returned to base without dropping its bomb. The last aircraft to attempt an attack on a Ruhr dam in Operation Chastise was Plt Off Bill Townsend in AJ-O. He dropped his bomb over the Ennepe dam at 0337 hr on his fourth attempt, but it failed to breach the wall.

Eleven Lancasters returned to Scampton as dawn was breaking, the last touching down at 0615 hr. Eight had failed to return, fifty-three crew were killed, and three were taken prisoner, making it a costly operation in terms of men and aircraft. The three Lancasters shot down after making their attacks were those of Maudslay, Young and Hopgood.

For his bravery in leading the raid and for distracting the flak defences away from subsequent attacks by his pilots, Guy Gibson was awarded the Victoria Cross. Thirty-three other aircrew received decorations for the roles they had played in the successful prosecution of the raid.

The force of the floodwaters as they bore down the valleys from the breaches in the Möhne and Eder dams was so great that the deafening waters swept away almost everything in their path. Homes were dashed to pieces, railway bridges torn down, trees uprooted, people and livestock carried away.

At 0730 hr on the morning of the 17th, a lone 542 Squadron Spitfire PR XI piloted by Flg Off Jerry Fray took off from Benson and headed for Germany and the Ruhr dams to photograph the results of the raids.

Several hundred miles ahead of Fray and his Spitfire, flooding along the Ruhr valley below the Möhne dam now extended for about 40 miles. The town of Neheim, which lay downstream from the dam itself, had been cut in half by the floodwaters.

About 150 miles from the Möhne dam, Fray could see the chemical haze that hung over the German industrial heartland of the Ruhr, and away to the east he noticed what he took to be a bank of cloud. As he flew closer it became apparent that this cloud was the effect of the sun glinting on the floodwaters some 30,000ft beneath him. Soon the enormity of the inundation that had hit the Ruhr valley became clear.

Eight hours after the attack, water was still gushing through the breach in the dam wall

Did You Know?

At the Ruhr valley's narrowest point, escaping water from the Möhne dam reached speeds of up to 18ft per second.

'We went back over the Möhne more from curiosity than anything. It was tremendous to see – an amazing sight I'll always remember. It was just like an inland sea. There was water everywhere in the moonlight, where before it had been a pretty reasonable valley.'

Sgt George Johnson, bomb aimer, AJ-T

◄◄

A breach 200ft across. Debris litters the compensating basin of the Möhne dam.
(Bundesarchiv)

A case of too little too late: a balloon barrage flies over the Möhne dam in this German photograph taken on 18 May. (Crown Copyright)

►► The upper reaches of the Möhne lake on 17 May, its brown mudbanks revealing that the reservoir is now virtually empty. (IWM CH9721)

at a rate of up to 70,000 cu ft/sec and the level of the water in the reservoir had fallen dramatically, leaving exposed brown mudflats around the edges. Fray carried out his photographic run over the Möhne before flying on to the Eder dam.

As he looked down from his Spitfire on to the virtually empty reservoir 6 miles beneath him, Fray observed that the damage in the Eder valley was far greater. This was largely because the breach in the dam was wider than that at the Möhne, allowing more than

The Eder dam photographed shortly after 617 Squadron's attack. (Crown Copyright)

➤➤
The sheer scale of the catastrophe that befell the Möhne is apparent from this photograph. (Bundesarchiv)

three-quarters of the contents of the reservoir to escape. The lake would have been impossible to pinpoint had it not been for the telltale white stain of water pouring from the breach in the dam wall. Two days after the attack, water was still gushing through it. Fray made a second run over the Eder to take further photographs, but, seeing two unidentified aircraft approaching from the north-east, he decided to cut short his sortie and beat it home.

'When I landed [the station commander] came up to me and said, "Have they hit them?" and I was able to answer, "Yes, they've pranged two of them properly. The floods are spreading for miles." So he went off to telephone the news to Bomber Command.'

Flg Off Jerry Fray, PR Spitfire pilot, 542 Squadron

Photoreconnaissance confirmed that material damage in both the Ruhr and Eder valleys was extensive, but was far more serious along the Möhne and Ruhr valleys. When Flg Off Jerry Fray landed his Spitfire back at RAF Benson in the mid-morning of 17 May with the first photographic intelligence of the raid, the feverish excitement that greeted him was palpable.
(Peter R. March)

At Benson the atmosphere was electric as the films were rushed from Fray's Spitfire and immediately developed. The first frames of negatives showed nothing but floodwater, but when the interpreters came to the Möhne dam, there was a gap right in the centre of the wall, about 200ft (60m) across, and water was pouring through it.

Once all the photographs had been printed and interpreted, it became very clear that the Möhne and Eder dams had been breached, but that the Sorpe was damaged and still intact. Benson despatched a further PR sortie at 1045 hr and a third one in the afternoon to add to the first coverage obtained by Fray.

Photoreconnaissance confirmed that material damage in both the Ruhr and Eder valleys was extensive, but was far more serious along the Möhne and Ruhr valleys. In places, the rivers had altered their courses and in time it would be necessary to divert them back along their old beds. In the shadow of the Möhne dam wall, the power station had been completely destroyed, along with the compensating basin, while the smaller power station situated a little further south was so seriously damaged as to be beyond repair. Further downstream, heavy damage had been caused to many more waterworks and power stations.

In the Ruhr valley, the weirs and mechanical plant at Echthausen and Wickede power stations had been totally destroyed. The weirs at Soest waterworks, Vereinigte Stahlwerke (steel works) and the power station at Fröndenberg had been wrecked, and large portions of the neighbouring canal bank had caved in. More than 5 miles of

overhead electric cables were also brought down in the area of Neheim and Fröndenberg. Further afield, the waterworks dam at Gelsenkirchen had been completely destroyed, and at Dortmund the waterworks and power station were badly damaged, causing huge disruption to heavy industry and domestic supplies in the area.

Thanks to the floodwaters, the transport network and its infrastructure along the Möhne and Ruhr valleys also suffered badly. The main railway line from Hagen to Kassel was seriously damaged between Neheim and Wickede, and in places the track bed was completely washed away. At Wickede the track itself had been lifted bodily off the embankment and washed on to the lower-lying fields below. It took until 11 June for express train services to be resumed. All road and narrow-gauge railway bridges in the

One of the massive water pipes used to feed the turbines of the main power station, destroyed by Hopgood's Upkeep weapon and then washed away by the floodwaters. (Bundesarchiv)

83

Floods swept away factory buildings in Neheim. The foundations in the foreground are all that remain. (RAF Museum)

Möhne valley were destroyed by the power of the floodwaters, and damage to roads was severe, ranging from potholes to the complete destruction of the roadbed and metalling.

Industry in the Möhne and Ruhr valleys was hard hit by the attack. Numerous firms lost buildings, machinery and materials, swept away by the floodwaters or seriously damaged by mud, and they were also

What remained of a detached house at Neheim that stood in the way of the floodwaters from the Möhne. Other houses were simply washed away.
(Bundesarchiv)

The Ruhr valley at Fröndenberg, 13 miles downstream from the Möhne. At 'A' stood a POW camp; at 'B', road and railway bridges that were swept away.
(Crown Copyright)

All that remained of the double-track steel railway bridge at Fröndenberg, ripped from its piers and carried more than 300ft downstream by the floodwaters.
(Bundesarchiv)

affected by damage to electricity and water supplies. The worst-hit area was the lower Möhne valley around Neheim: the steel works at Hagen-Kabel and Harkort-Eicken in Wetter was extensively damaged by the effects of the attack.

Downstream from the Eder dam, the villages of Hemfurth, Affoldern, Mehlen, Bergheim and Giflitz were badly affected by the floodwaters, while several miles further on, the Luftwaffe airfield at Fritzlar was completely flooded. Twenty-five road and rail bridges had been swept away, including the railway station at Giflitz and the bridge carrying the main line to Frankfurt. Serious inundations affected Hemfurth and Affoldern, as well as parts of the city of Kassel. In fact, the effects of the flooding were felt in the Fulda and Weser rivers for a distance of about 300 miles from the Eder. At Hameln, more than 130 miles away, the River Weser rose by more than 20ft (6m) in the immediate aftermath of the raid.

The death toll among the population of the Ruhr valley was 1,294, although some German sources believe it to be in excess of 1,400. Some 493 were Ukrainian women – forced labourers – although Dutch, French and Belgian prisoners of war were also among the casualties. Three months later, as the clearing-up operation continued, bodies were still being found at Neheim.

By noon on the 17th the floodwaters had abated in Neheim and Wickede, but the Ruhr valley itself had been shorn of all its familiar features by the scouring effect of the fast-moving water.

Shortly before the raid, water production in the Ruhr stood at 1 million cubic metres per day. Although this figure plummeted by

three-quarters in its aftermath, within six weeks the original output had been restored. Water supplies to the city of Dortmund fell to one-fifth in a matter of hours after the raid; within three days they were back up to four-fifths.

Electricity supplies were also only temporarily disrupted. It was not necessary to rebuild the power station at the Möhne, and the giant power plant at Herdecke was only offline for a fortnight. In any case, the Germans obtained alternative electricity supplies from generating stations that used water from the Alps.

At first sight, heavy industry appeared to have been largely unaffected: steel production in the Greater Reich and the occupied territories actually exceeded that of 1942 by 2.5 million tons. However, the important waterworks at Fröndenberg and Echthausen were disabled in the early hours of the 17th and were not returned to full working order until August. The Ruhr suffered an 8 per cent drop in steel output in the second half of

Did You Know?
The RAF missed a second opportunity to cause mayhem in the Ruhr valley while the Germans were engaged in rebuilding the Möhne and Eder dams. A few bombs would have produced cave-ins at the exposed building sites, and a few firebombs could have set the wooden scaffolding blazing.

◄
By 10 a.m. on 17 May, the floodwaters of the Eder lake had reached the city of Kassel, 37 miles downstream.
(Crown Copyright)

'The RAF came close to a success which would have been greater than anything they had achieved hitherto with a commitment of thousands of bombers.'

Albert Speer, Hitler's Armaments Minister

1943, while the whole of north-west Germany lost 1.9 million tons of crude steel production that year. The loss of vital water supplies to coke works in the Ruhr valley also meant that supplies to principal gas consumers were slashed by more than half on 19 May.

Rebuilding of the Möhne and Eder dams proceeded quickly and, on 25 September, the gap in the Möhne's wall was finally closed, while work on the Eder was completed soon afterwards. However, it was not until 1946–7 that they were able to operate at full capacity once more.

Nor was it only industry that suffered the consequences of the attacks. Agriculture and food supplies were hit, too. The scouring effect of the floodwaters stripped away topsoil on farmland in the Möhne and Eder valleys, rendering them virtually impossible to cultivate, and they remained barren for many years to come.

The diversion of labour and resources to repair the damage caused by the raids was short-term, but 10,000 men were seconded to build and man defences at dams considered at risk of future air attack. It represented a longer-term drain on both civilian and military resources.

The question of how best to protect Germany's dams was considered at length. At the Möhne dam, the results included additional torpedo nets, special Luftwaffe fighter cover, 328ft-high aerial steel curtains stretched across the reservoir to deter low-flying aircraft, and anti-bomb and anti-rocket netting projecting out from the wall on the dam's air side. This was in addition to searchlights, barrage balloons and smokescreen equipment. Extensive provision for the

defence of the Eder and Sorpe dams was also made.

The effect on civilian morale of the attacks in the Ruhr and Eder valleys is difficult to gauge. Allied bombing of the Ruhr had been going on for many years, with particular intensity between March and July 1943 in the so-called Battle of the Ruhr, during which time the RAF mounted thirty-one major raids. It is therefore difficult to separate the effects of the general bombing of the region from the specific civilian response to the dams raids. Much clearing up and rebuilding of homes had to be undertaken in the aftermath of the floods, but civilian wrath was not simply confined to Britain and the RAF.

The competence of the Luftwaffe was called into question, since defensive measures to protect the dams were so obviously lacking. A devastating attack on the dams from the air had been considered an impossibility by the German military.

For German Intelligence, something quite unexpected came out of the raids – an intact Upkeep bomb. This was the weapon from Flt Lt Bob Barlow's Lancaster, AJ-E, which had rolled clear of the blazing wreckage, relatively undamaged. It was successfully defused and thoroughly examined by the authorities. The Luftwaffe came close to uncovering the secrets of Barnes Wallis's bouncing bomb and, by September 1943, they were carrying out basic tests on a design of their own. But the critical detail they failed to discover was the depth at which the bomb was supposed to explode, and that it had to explode in contact with the dam wall to be effective.

Harris, Cochrane and Wallis had followed the unfolding drama of the night in the tense atmosphere of the operations room at 5 Group HQ, Grantham. When they received the code word 'Nigger' at 0056 hr, indicating that the Möhne dam had been breached, followed by 'Dinghy' at 0154 hr to confirm that the Eder, too, had been breached, there were scenes of intense jubilation in the ops room. At 0400 hr a car took Harris, Cochrane and Wallis to Scampton, where they joined the surviving crews of the first wave who were being debriefed.

Once debriefing was over, the crews retired to the mess for bacon and eggs and stood at the bar waiting for the others to arrive. But it eventually became clear that eight aircraft were missing and their crews would not be coming home. Gibson left early to help the adjutant, Flt Lt Humphries, and

'Chiefy' Powell with the fifty-six casualty telegrams to next of kin. On the morning of the 18th, the men of 617 Squadron went on some well-earned leave.

Meanwhile, across Britain, the first reports of the operation were heard on the BBC radio news on the morning of the 17th, and the initial press coverage followed the same day in the regional evening newspapers. It was

Gibson's crew are debriefed after the raid, while Harris and Cochrane look on. From left to right: Harris, Townson (intelligence officer), Spafford, Cochrane, Taerum and Trevor-Roper.
(IWM CH9683)

'In the early hours of this morning, a force of Lancasters attacked with mines the dams at the Möhne and Sorpe reservoirs. The Eder dam was also attacked and reported as breached. The attacks were pressed home from a very low level with great determination and coolness in the face of fierce resistance.'

Air Ministry communiqué, 17 May 1943

The surviving aircraft captains are caught on camera outside the officers' mess at Scampton. Back row, left to right: Townsend (AJ-O), McCarthy (AJ-T), Wilson (did not fly, because of illness in his crew), Gibson (AJ-G), Munro (AJ-W), Maltby (AJ-J), Brown (AJ-F). Front row: Anderson (AJ-Y), Rice (AJ-H), Martin (AJ-F), Shannon (AJ-L), Knight (AJ-N).
(RAF Museum)

not until the 18th that the nationals went to town on coverage.

To a blitz-weary nation with little in the way of good news to celebrate since the British victory at El Alamein the previous autumn, this daring raid deep into the Nazi heartland by RAF Bomber Command struck a chord.

News of the attacks provoked a favourable response from Britain's allies overseas, in Soviet Russia, the occupied countries of Europe and in particular the USA. Here it came at a timely point in the Trident Conference, and was widely and positively reported in the media. Up to this point, there were many in North America who had been expressing doubts about the effectiveness of Bomber Command's campaign, as well as that of their own 8th Air Force. Chastise gave Churchill the propaganda coup he was looking for, and at just the right time.

To 617 Squadron, Operation Chastise was not without its cost in human terms. The operation claimed the lives of fifty-

'With one single blow the RAF has precipitated what may prove to be the greatest industrial disaster yet inflicted on Germany in this war. Today walls of water sweeping down the Ruhr and Eder valleys are carrying everything before them.'
Daily Telegraph, 18 May 1943

Did You Know?
Operation Chastise claimed the lives of fifty-three aircrew from 617 Squadron. The youngest RAF airman to die on the raid was 18-year-old Sgt Jack Liddell, rear gunner in Flt Lt Bob Barlow's crew, whose Lancaster crashed on the outward flight.

three men, many of whom, like Hopgood, Maudslay and Young, were highly experienced bomber pilots and impossible to replace.

On 24 May details of the decorations awarded to 617 Squadron's aircrew were passed on to the squadron, before they were officially announced in the supplement to the

With a scale model of the Möhne dam before him, the King shares a joke with Gibson, while Cochrane and Whitworth look on. (IWM CH9924)

On 27 May the King and Queen visited Scampton to review 617 Squadron's air and ground crews. (IWM CH9950)

➤
*Wg Cdr Guy Gibson
stands smartly to
attention for the royal
inspection.* (IWM TR1002)

Did You Know?
Wg Cdr Guy Gibson was awarded the Victoria Cross and thirty-three aircrew members of the squadron received gallantry decorations: five Distinguished Service Orders; four Bars to the Distinguished Flying Cross (DFC); ten DFCs; two Conspicuous Gallantry Medals; one bar to the Distinguished Flying Medal (DFM); and eleven DFMs.

London Gazette the next day. Gibson received the Victoria Cross, and thirty-three members of the squadron were awarded gallantry decorations in recognition of their part in Chastise, making 617 the most decorated squadron in the RAF.

The publicity that followed the raid continued unabated. On the 27th the King and Queen paid a royal visit to Scampton; on 21 June, 617's air and ground crews

Flt Lt Mick Martin meets the King, as Whitworth, Gibson and Cochrane look on. (IWM CH9928)

'The day after the raid we were pretty stunned when we saw the lorries coming along the [billets] to pick up the effects of the ones who were gone. Until then we didn't realise it had been so many.'
Flt Sgt Grant McDonald, rear gunner, AJ-F

travelled to London for their investiture by the Queen at Buckingham Palace the following day. On the evening of the 22nd, a celebratory dinner was hosted by A.V. Roe & Co. Ltd, builders of the Lancaster, at the Hungaria Restaurant in Lower Regent Street. In addition to 617 Squadron personnel, Roy Chadwick, designer of the Lancaster,

Following their
investiture at
Buckingham Palace,
Taerum, Spafford, Trevor-
Roper, Maltby, Gibson,
Johnson, Martin,
Shannon, Hobday and
McCarthy pose for the
camera. (IWM HU62923)

On 22 June, A.V. Roe &
Co. hosted a celebratory
dinner at the Hungaria
Restaurant on London's
Lower Regent Street to
mark the investiture of
617's personnel by the
Queen. (RAF Museum)

Barnes Wallis and other personalities from
Vickers were also present.

Guy Gibson achieved celebrity status in
the months that followed, although to begin
with he was something of a reluctant hero.

Morale-boosting visits to war factories across
Britain were followed by an invitation from
the Prime Minister, Winston Churchill, to
accompany him to Canada in August for the
Quebec Conference. After the conference,

'No one believed that we should do it. You yourself said it would be a miracle if we did, and I think the whole thing is one of the most amazing examples of teamwork and co-operation in the whole history of the war.'

Barnes Wallis to Roy Chadwick,

25 May 1943

104

Gibson with an almost complete line-up of surviving 617 Squadron aircrew, pictured after the raid. (RAF Museum)

Australian survivors of the dams raid. From left to right: Hay (AJ-P), Howard (AJ-O), Shannon (AJ-L), Leggo (AJ-P), Spafford (AJ-G), Martin (AJ-P), Knight (AJ-N), Kellow (AJ-N). Not in this photograph are Foxlee and Simpson, who also survived the raid, and Burcher, who became a POW. (IWM CH9936)

 Canadian survivors of the dams raid. Standing, from left to right: Oancia (AJ-F), Sutherland (AJ-N), O'Brien (AJ-N), Brown (AJ-F), Weeks (AJ-W), Thrasher (AJ-H), Deering (AJ-G), Radcliffe (AJ-T), MacLean (AJ-T), McCarthy (AJ-T), McDonald (AJ-F). Front: Pigeon (AJ-W), Taerum (AJ-G), Walker (AJ-L), Gowrie (AJ-H), Rodger (AJ-T). (IWM CH9935)

▶▶
The Möhne and the Eder dams pictured today. The Eder's walls bear signs of the repairs to the breach, where the overflow sluices have been omitted. (Richard Simms/Eder-Touristic)

there followed a gruelling four-month-long public relations tour of Canada and the USA. Arriving back in England during December, Gibson's hopes of being allowed to return to operations were dashed when he was officially grounded and posted to a desk job at the Air Ministry in January 1944.

But the Guy Gibson story does not end there. In the months that followed, he wrote a book about his experiences as a bomber pilot, which was published posthumously in 1946 as *Enemy Coast Ahead*. Under the patronage of Winston Churchill, he was selected as the prospective Conservative

parliamentary candidate for Macclesfield, but withdrew his candidacy in August, desperate to get back on operations. He wangled his way back to operational flying and, on 19/20 September 1944, he flew in a 627 Squadron Mosquito as master bomber on a raid against Rheydt and Mönchengladbach. On the way home, the Mosquito crashed in Holland, killing Gibson and the navigator, Sqn Ldr J.B. Warwick. Exactly why the Mosquito crashed remains a mystery.

Following the dams raid, 617 Squadron went from strength to strength. With its reputation for precision bombing it continued to be employed on special missions until the war's end. Its Lancasters were further modified to carry Barnes Wallis's 'super bombs' – the 12,000lb Tallboy and latterly the 22,000lb Grand Slam, which were used to breach the Dortmund–Ems canal, sink the much-feared German battleship *Tirpitz*, and bring down the Arnsberg viaduct, among many other operations.

In the twenty-first century, the legend of 617 Squadron lives on with the 1,452mph Panavia Tornado GR4 bomber, capable of carrying up to 18,000lb of ordnance. Ironically, the Tornado was developed and built by a European consortium of manufacturers that includes Britain and Germany.

◄ *Panavia Tornados are 617 Squadron's twenty-first century successors to the Lancasters of the war years. This is a Tornado GR4 bearing the squadron's markings beneath the cockpit and on the fin.* (Peter R. March)

APPENDIX I – AVRO LANCASTER BIII (TYPE 464 PROVISIONING)

Type: four-engine, seven-man mid-wing monoplane heavy night bomber

Power plant: 4 × 1,480hp Packard-built Rolls-Royce Merlin 28 12-cylinder, liquid-cooled, in-line, supercharged engines

Performance: 287mph (462km/h) at 11,500ft, cruising speed 210mph (338km/h) at 12,000ft, service ceiling 24,500ft (without bomb load), range 1,660 miles (2,670km) with 14,000lb bomb load

Length: 69ft 6in (21.18m)

Wingspan: 102ft 0in (31.09m)

Wing area: 1,297 sq ft (120.5m²)

Height: 20ft 4in (6.20m)

Armament:

Defensive 2 × 0.303in Browning machine guns in Frazer-Nash FN5 nose turret
4 × 0.303in Browning machine guns in Frazer-Nash FN20 tail turret
1 × 0.303in Vickers K gun in ventral downward-firing position

Offensive 1 × 9,250lb Upkeep bouncing bomb

Weights: 36,457lb (16,537kg) empty, 68,000lb (30,845kg) loaded

Key: FE = flight engineer; N = navigator;
W/Op = wireless operator; BA = bomb aimer;
FG = front gunner; RG = rear gunner

SQUADRON COMMANDER: WG CDR G.P. GIBSON, DSO AND BAR, DFC AND BAR, AJ-G, ED932/G

Crew: Sgt J. Pulford DFM (FE), Plt Off T.H. Taerum DFC (Nav), Flt Lt E.G. Hutchison DFC and Bar (W/Op), Plt Off F.M. Spafford DFC (BA), Flt Sgt G.A. Deering DFC, RCAF (FG), Flt Lt.A.D. Trevor-Roper DFC (RG)

FLT LT J.V. HOPGOOD DFC AND BAR (CAPTAIN), AJ-M, ED925/G

Crew: Sgt C. Brennan (FE), Flg Off K. Earnshaw RCAF (N), Sgt J.W. Minchin (W/Op), Plt Off J.W. Fraser DFM (BA), Plt Off G.H.F.G. Gregory DFM (FG), Plt Off A.F. Burcher DFM, RAAF (RG)

FLT LT H.B. MARTIN DFC (CAPTAIN), AJ-P, ED909/G

Crew: Plt Off I. Whittaker (FE), Flt Lt J.F. Leggo DFC, RAAF (N), Flg Off L. Chambers RNZAF (W/Op), Flt Lt R.C. Hay DFC, RAAF (BA), Plt Off T.B. Foxlee DFM, RAAF (FG), Flt Sgt T.D. Simpson RAAF (RG)

SQN LDR H.M. YOUNG DFC AND BAR (CAPTAIN), AJ-A, ED877/G

Crew: Sgt D.T. Horsfall (FE), Flt Sgt C.W. Roberts (N), Sgt L.W. Nichols (W/Op), Flt Lt V.S. MacCausland RCAF (BA), Sgt G.A. Yeo (FG), Sgt W. Ibbotson (RG)

FLT LT D.J. MALTBY DFC (CAPTAIN), AJ-J, ED906/G

Crew: Sgt W. Hatton (FE), Sgt V. Nicholson (N), Sgt A.J.B. Stone (W/Op), Plt Off J. Fort (BA), Sgt V. Hill (FG), Sgt H.T. Simmonds (RG)

FLT LT D. SHANNON DFC, RAAF (CAPTAIN), AJ-L, ED929/G

Crew: Sgt R.J. Henderson (FE), Flg Off D.R. Walker DFC, RCAF (N), Flg Off B. Goodale DFC (W/Op), Flt Sgt L.J. Sumpter (BA), Sgt B. Jagger (FG), Flg Off J. Buckley (RG)

SQN LDR H.E. MAUDSLAY DFC (CAPTAIN), AJ-Z, ED937/G

Crew: Sgt J. Marriot (FE), Flg Off R.A. Urquhart (N), WO II A.P. Cottam (W/Op), Plt Off M.J.D. Fuller (BA), Flg Off J. Tytherleigh (FG), Sgt N.R. Burrows (RG)

FLT LT W. ASTELL DFC (CAPTAIN), AJ-B, ED864/G

Crew: Sgt J. Kinnear (FE), Plt Off F.A. Wile (N), WO II A. Garshowitz (W/Op), Flg Off D. Hopkinson (BA), Flt Sgt F.A. Garbas (FG), Sgt R. Bolitho (RG)

PLT OFF L.G. KNIGHT RAAF (CAPTAIN), AJ-N, ED912/G

Crew: Sgt R.E. Grayston (FE), Flg Off H.S. Hobday (N), Flt Sgt R.G.T. Kellow (W/Op), Flg Off E.C. Johnson (BA), Sgt F.E. Sutherland (FG), Sgt H.E. O'Brien (RG)

FLT LT R.N.G. BARLOW DFC, RAAF (CAPTAIN), AJ-E, ED927/G

Crew: P/O S.L. Whillis (FE), Flg Off P.S. Burgess (N), Flg Off C.R. Williams DFC, RAAF (W/Op), Plt Off A. Gillespie DFM (BA), Flg Off H.S. Glinz RCAF (FG), Sgt J.R.G. Liddell (RG)

FLT LT J.L. MUNRO RNZAF (CAPTAIN), AJ-W, ED921/G

Crew: Sgt F.E. Appleby (FE), Flg Off F.G. Rumbles (N), Sgt P.E. Pigeon (W/Op), Sgt J.H. Clay (BA), Sgt W. Howarth (FG), Flt Sgt H.A. Weeks (RG)

PLT OFF V.W. BYERS RCAF (CAPTAIN), AJ-K, ED934/G

Crew: Sgt A.J. Taylor (FE), Flt Off J.H. Warner (N), Sgt J. Wilkinson (W/Op), Plt Off A.N. Whitaker (BA), Sgt C. McA. Jarvie (FG), Flt Sgt McDowell (RG)

PLT OFF G. RICE (CAPTAIN), AJ-H, ED936/G

Crew: Sgt E.C. Smith (FE), Flg Off R. MacFarlane (N), Sgt C.B. Gowrie (W/Op), Flt Sgt J.W. Thrasher (BA), Sgt T.W. Maynard (FG), Sgt S. Burns (RG)

FLT LT J.C. McCARTHY DFC, RCAF (CAPTAIN), AJ-T, ED825/G

Crew: Sgt W. Radcliffe (FE), Flt Sgt D.A. MacLean (N), Sgt L. Eaton (W/Op), Sgt G.L. Johnson (BA), Sgt R. Batson (FG), Flg Off D. Rodger (RG)

PLT OFF W.H.T. OTTLEY DFC (CAPTAIN), AJ-C, ED910/G

Crew: Sgt R. Marsden (FE), Flg Off J.K. Barrett (N), Sgt J. Guterman (W/Op), Flt Sgt T.B. Johnston (BA), Sgt F. Tees (FG), Sgt H.J. Strange (RG)

PLT OFF L.J. BURPEE DFM, RCAF (CAPTAIN), AJ-S, ED865/G

Crew: Sgt G. Pegler (FE), Sgt T. Jaye (N), Plt Off L.G. Weller (W/Op), WO II J.L. Arthur (BA), Sgt W.C.A. Long (FG), WO II J.G. Brady (RG)

FLT SGT K.W. BROWN RCAF (CAPTAIN), AJ-F, ED918/G

Crew: Sgt H.B. Feneron (FE), Sgt D.P. Heal (N), Sgt H.J. Hewstone (W/Op), Sgt S. Oancia (BA), Sgt D. Allatson (FG), Flt Sgt G.S. McDonald (RG)

PLT OFF W.C. TOWNSEND DFM (CAPTAIN), AJ-O, ED886/G

Crew: Sgt D.J.D. Powell (FE), Plt Off C.L. Howard (N), Flt Sgt A. Chalmers (W/Op), Sgt C.E. Franklin (BA), Sgt D.E. Webb (FG), Sgt R. Wilkinson (RG)

FLT SGT C.T. ANDERSON (CAPTAIN), AJ-Y, ED924/G

Crew: Sgt R.C. Patterson (FE), Sgt J.P. Nugent (N), Sgt W.D. Bickle (W/Op), Sgt G.J. Green (BA), Sgt E. Ewan (FG), Sgt A.W. Buck (RG)

The name of Plt Off V.W. Byers appears on the Allied Air Forces Memorial, Runnymede.

HOPGOOD CREW, AJ-M, ED925/G

Damaged by flak on its approach to the Möhne dam, then caught in the blast from its Upkeep weapon, which had overshot the parapet and exploded on the air side of the dam. Crashed at 0034 hr at Ostonnen, 3¾ miles east of Werl, Germany. Five killed. Two crew survived to become POWs: Plt Off Jim Fraser RCAF and Plt Off Anthony Burcher DFM, RAAF.

YOUNG CREW, AJ-A, ED877/G

Shot down by flak crossing the Dutch coast on the return flight, and crashed at 0258 hr off Castricum-aan-Zee, Netherlands. All killed.

MAUDSLAY CREW, AJ-Z, ED937/G

Badly damaged over the Möhne dam by the detonation of its own Upkeep weapon and hit by flak on the return flight. Crashed at 0236 hr at Netterden, 1¾ miles east of Emmerich, Germany. All killed.

ASTELL CREW, AJ-B, ED864/G

Flew into high-tension cables and pylon on the outward flight near Marbeck, 3 miles SSE of Borken, Germany. Crashed at 0015 hr. All killed.

BARLOW CREW, AJ-E, ED927/G

Flew into high-tension cables on the outward flight at Haldern, 2½ miles ENE of Rees, Germany. Crashed at 2350 hr. All killed.

BYERS CREW, AJ-K, ED934/G

Hit by flak on the outward flight from batteries on the Dutch island of Texel and crashed into the Waddenzee, west of Harlingen (precise time unknown). All killed.

OTTLEY CREW, AJ-C, ED910/G

Hit by flak on the outward flight and crashed on the Boserlagerschenwald near Hessen, 1¾ miles NNE of Hamm, Germany, at 0235 hr. Six killed. Sgt Fred Tees survived as a POW.

BURPEE CREW, AJ-S, ED865/G

Hit by flak on the outward flight and crashed at 0200 hr near Gilze-Rijen airfield, Netherlands. All killed.

ABORTED SORTIES

FLT LT J.L. MUNRO RNZAF, AJ-W, ED921/G

Hit by light flak on the outward flight crossing Vlieland, Holland, damaging the VHF radio and intercom. Landed back at Scampton 0030 hr with mine still on board.

PLT OFF G. RICE, AJ-H, ED936/G

Hit the sea on the outward flight near Vlieland, ripping off the Upkeep mine and tearing a hole in the bomb bay. Landed back at Scampton 0050 hr.

FLT SGT C.T. ANDERSON, AJ-Y, ED924/G

The Anderson crew experienced navigational difficulties and malfunction of rear turret. Turned back over Germany at 0310 hr without dropping mine. Landed back at Scampton 0530 hr with mine still on board.